Starlight Hear

Copyright @2023 Elise
All rights reserved.
No part of this book may be reproduced
or used in any manner without
written permission of the copyright owner
except for the use of quotations in a book review.

Poetry

Journey into a starlight world full of starlight heart's.
Loss, pain, change, courage, and transformation.
A testament to the strength of our own hearts,
that go through life with us, still beating.
Poems from one starlight heart to another…

For the starlight in our hearts that never fades

dear heart,
it's you and me now

aberrant beauty
divergent in all aspects of her being
a cosmic girl covered in fortitude
and wondrous tales

flowers blooming in my heart
bursting stars into life
from the rubble
of our love

she stopped looking outside
and turned her gaze inside
to find a whole world of herself

Starlight Heart | Elise

whispers from her heart
could light up any dark
if only she has the courage
to listen to their beat

Starlight Heart | Elise

she's got a heart
glowing with
midnight music

she felt in her mind
a devastating renewal
and the game changed

she learned to love
her creative process
to do, to act in a way
that would change
her mindset
she found dancing
to her music
the best way to
electrolyze the
creative juices
and capture
the energy of
imagination
and combine
it with her
own personal
experience
thus far in
the journey of life
she moves in her truth
and then she writes

Starlight Heart | Elise

you can keep your words
show me the actions
from the rhythm
of your heart

block out the noise of it all
run with the song in your soul

you can talk of the matrix
but the true ruin of a person
is not becoming who you
dream to be, who you can be
how curious that
in pain we find
transcendence
and transformation
and we finally wear
the fiery colours of our feathers
shimmering in our own sunlight
because we realise
we won't die without that person
we will live, and we will live
with ourselves for eternity

I thought I knew it all
I thought I knew the programming
in the energy of the world
maybe I knew enough to get me started
but I didn't know the depths of pain
that heartbreak would bring me
and I didn't know the lengths
I would travel, to heal myself
and I didn't know the glorious
nature of change
that the agony would
bring with it

the truth is
I went searching for
all the answers outside of me
before I even looked at the deep
mystery of my own heart

Starlight Heart | Elise

the stars in my brain
seem to be smiling
at the person
I am becoming now

the work that you do
to transform yourself
is the most valuable

ride on stallions of spirits
into the mist of nightmares
and master holding on
and letting go
until the art of life is
a dance and a song

Starlight Heart | Elise

I taste in my mind
a song never sung
where the lyrics bloom
from the hearts of the young

Starlight Heart | Elise

I let it get so dark in my mind
I lost my way
straying from the road
I'd felt in my heart as a little girl
I'd gone into the underworld
of my conscious mind and
traded parts of me to the dragon
that resides there
for something I'd let everyone else
convince me I needed
but the darkness of Tartarus
left me only with myself
because I realised I must
first conquer myself
and know every part of me
for what I have become
and dream again
for all that I can become

you came to me in my dreams
as a blue fox,
rolling around in midnight dust
your smile invited me into the woods
your sanctuary of nocturnal wonders
and unusual trinkets

endless neon butterflies
flew out of my soul
into life
and I thought
so this is my true form

none before you
have struck a chord
where you had in my heart
and brought to life music
that I didn't know I had
inside me

in the opera of my heart
flutes
harps
pianos
electronic sounds
play in perfect tune
a song I'd only heard
in my dreams
now the more I bloom
the louder it plays

Starlight Heart | Elise

it's time to say I set the tone
I carved the stars from my heart
and it was the breath from my lungs
that began to sing

Starlight Heart | Elise

by the talking campfire
the constellation of stars dancing
to the owl's song
I came here one last time
to leave a note
in the forest of fables
and fairy folk and freedom

your words hit home
more than you know

Starlight Heart | Elise

I've always belonged
to the travelling festival
of dreams, the abnormal
the rare
the ones who beat with
a different sound
make it out of this town
they ask me, but I've always known
it's a feeling that has grown and grown
it's light in the deepest ocean
speaking words once unspoken
reminding me, my life is rectifiable
the light I can't ignore, undeniable

now fate has sent us separate ways
but I'll always feel connected by an
invisible string from your soul to mine

butterfly in flames
lightning in flowers

a cup of the universe
drink raspberry
swirls and sugar
plums and nectar
dreams and desires
coated deeply in
imaginations dust
and dripped in
soul music
cheers

the only thing that kept me alive
was knowing that I had this untold
story inside of me that I needed to tell

she's different from the others
she walks down by the river
every night into the darkness
between the stars
and converses with herself
as the night goes on
the little creatures
of the forest
the gnomes and goblins
and fairies or whatever name
you give them
gather to watch her
this strange girl, this different girl,
this mysterious girl
this girl with the stars in her heart

in a way it has set me free
and I'm sure I'll thank you
for it eventually
but right now, I'm playing
a tune to my song

Starlight Heart | Elise

what if the greatest achievement is in
becoming all that you can be
what if the person you become
on pursuit of your goals
is the real prize

Starlight Heart | Elise

I'm starting to think the thoughts
that linger in abandoned buildings
the rare thoughts that grow
in the first rays of light
new and alive
and full of infinite possibilities

Starlight Heart | Elise

her energy is like a cloak she wears
in her heart, protecting her mind from
the noise, the only noise that matters
the only sound in her ears she will permit
is the sound of her own song
thrumming through her veins

as a child you knew
you'd go a different way
your way
you are a warrior
until the sun goes down
then you're a lover

Starlight Heart | Elise

it's only after,
I realised I had
lost the thoughts
I used to cherish,
the dreams
a vital process of
reinventing myself
in fires and stars
began to materialize
through the pain
emerging from the night
with a brighter light

move how you want to be darling
fly like an eagle, roar like a tiger
dream like a poet
live like your best self
and that's what
you'll become

spirit animal of the southern wind
fly with wings of starlight

in the cocoon of change
transformation seeps into your blood
and the new you looks good on you

you will find the will to keep going

you either know you have it in you or you don't

now I'm alone
but I've got her
the girl in my stories
the girl who's been with me
since I can remember
she's a part of me
as real as the stars above
and the stars inside

he was a different kind of musician
he could play the waves energy in the air
sound frequency, vibration,
he could play the electricity in the air
and so could I

bring the golden fire
that is abundant
inside of you

it was too loud
everything was too loud
and I didn't pay attention
to the song
running like an underground river
beneath my skin
like a hidden railroad in a cave
under the surface of the Earth
of my body
distant horns become vibrant
as I ride the express along
the track to the stars
I'm listening now

only you can do this now

Starlight Heart | Elise

I'd got sidetracked from my purpose
what I knew I was here to do
to see how far I can go
and meeting you
was a ripple in the water
I could taste the sweetness of
your passion for your
own musical ventures
from the beginning,
I admired that about you
and I always will
and now it's set off
my dream in me again
I wish you good fortune to
all the stars in your heart

the ones that understand
the unending depth of a dream
you see, I've always known
a writer, a storyteller,
a conjurer of words
a deep diver explorer
of imagination and beyond
stories are in my bones
and the pull is so strong
success is the only option
and masterpieces are inevitable

to write an exceptional story
I must first become exceptional

Starlight Heart | Elise

you think I'm alone
but writers never are
we've got a constant
parade of vivid
characters and storylines
and a world of wonder
inside our heads

because when you step into yourself
and live with your energy
and your own harmony
instead of anyone else's
that's when the universe
recognises you
and you recognise yourself
truly step into your power

if you are with yourself
in every way
the universe is with you also

Starlight Heart | Elise

as a young girl
I think I fell in love
with my stories
before anyone else

and then it was a flood of memories
and the heartbreak made all the words
come pouring out of me in the water
of what was left of me
a catalyst of rapid change,
I transformed myself
I knew I had to kiss goodbye to who I was
and throw my heart into what I would now become
like painting a new picture, landscape, and portrait
with my tears, with the blood from my broken heart
with all the new wisdom, with all the lessons learnt
a devastatingly honest process of
renewal, remaking, and reworking
inventing, building, and designing
a magnum opus of myself
and I realised it's true
your soul is your greatest work of art

who you've become through it all
the person you've made yourself into
that's the real gold

let this promise in me bloom
like flowers on fire
and my veins are rivers of fuel
that carry ammunition to my heart
fire away

and the paintings came alive
on her skin,
like a map of vivid tattoos
telling an intricate story that
was as old as time but as vibrant
as a beating heart
so this is what it feels like to truly live

Starlight Heart | Elise

drinking a brew of the universe
her own special batch
most nights she'd drink
straight from the sky's stream
but tonight she added her own
crafted potions
of raspberry heart
the will to keep going
and a touch of self-proclaimed destiny

sometimes you can tell
who has just dipped
their toe into greatness
and who has
forged themselves
in the flames of suffering
and risen to success

Starlight Heart | Elise

strawberry cake
sweet as the memory of you
celebrate on bonfire night
fireworks and caramel apples
moments that built a castle in my mind
I lit the fire and burnt what I must let go of
and I watched the bonfire kiss the sky
and I thought of you
a ghost that's still alive

all the stories in her mind
her heart, her soul
burst from their astral realm
and engraved themselves onto her flesh
curious, they have a mind of their own
would they be a different form without me
would I be different without them

Starlight Heart | Elise

she inked her poems on her skin
she became her poetry
the girl of ink and stars and stories

in the darkness of your heart,
can you look at yourself
in the pain-stained mirror
and recognise the reflection

Starlight Heart | Elise

though the fire around me raged like
an unyielding storm
battering against my ship since the day
I was born
try as you might to destroy my will
my own fire burns brighter still
poison words and whispered lies
I won't listen, I'll still rise

set sail
I pull my boat
and anchor into the starry sea
my heart beats to the story
farewell traveller in my dreams
whatever it takes, I shall not fail
set sail, set sail

Starlight Heart | Elise

hold out a light
light the lanterns
and watch them take flight
leaving the shore
more prepared than before
riding the winds of the world
a story of a girl
found her way in darkness
with the hum of a song
always singing inside
turn the lights on

it may seem like you'll never fly after this
but I promise you, you will fly with diamonds on your wings
for what is a diamond if it were not forged under pressure

she's in the process
of alchemical transmutation
transfiguration of her heart

Starlight Heart | Elise

it's too painful to stay the same
now my best friend is change
progress made with a broken heart
to know the light you must know the dark

Starlight Heart | Elise

weary traveller
the journey's been far
and her heart will be light
and her eyes will fill with stars

a tale of adventure and choices
for which I will not apologise
all I have done, is the ink
on the paper from the story of my life

Starlight Heart | Elise

fly away butterfly
you are your own salvation

Starlight Heart | Elise

she came in the night like a firefly
when the chime plays at midnight
under shooting stars light
never forget the sparkling in her eyes
she came in the night like those fireflies

now light up the sky with your eternal flame
write among the stars your true name

and at the end of it all
you will find her
at the edge of the world
writing in her book
smiling to the world
and her eyes will fill with stars

Starlight Heart | Elise

under the shine of the stars
amongst the vastness of the desert
bursts of colourful light shot into the night sky
and at its source, a girl, dreaming while awake
sending out her signal fire

Starlight Heart | Elise

she raised a glass to the darkness
to the ones who make their dreams
come true

Starlight Heart | Elise

I'll meet you in the whispers of a fairytale
in the bright light of ideas
in the tears of hearts
and in the hope before you bring yourself back to life

Starlight Heart | Elise

I'm talking to the ones
who carry starlight inside them
you shine with a rarer glow

Starlight Heart | Elise

every soul has her own song
and when you find another's song
that matches so perfectly with your own
you know you were made for each other

Starlight Heart | Elise

dream of me tonight
and when the wheel chimes at midnight
I'll meet you there, in your dreams

wanderer, vagabond, king of the journey
travelling to distant lands
in search of yourself
a road map to the stars
etched across your heart
you leave lanterns on the cobbled stones
when our paths cross, we meet our match
don't look back
legendary times lay ahead
it's meant to be
I'll meet you, when we've both
become who we are meant to be

•

a woman's heart carries deep secrets
lovers, lust, nights of passion, nights of despair
moments of strength and moments of weakness
memories, hopes, dreams
she may choose to share her secrets with a man
if he has touched her heart
but some secrets she will not whisper a word
the secrets meant for only her to know
how much she really loved him
they remain locked away
buried inside a chest that lives
at the very bottom of the ocean in her heart

we found each other's gaze across the camp fire
eyes meeting, sparking a ripple through the world
one look was all it took

her first love was her stories
then the night
you'll find her at midnight
tears streaming down her face
mind dreaming of a story untold
gazing whole-heartedly at the night
and her treasured stars

forever you will stay in my heart
as I stare up at the stars you are all I see

I'm seeking something only I can give to myself

the stars listened to every breath she took
and every story she shared

Starlight Heart | Elise

you could imagine her
dancing naked under the stars
while the campfire blew embers
saluting her great unyielding love for life

lucid dreaming
sipping on starlight
late night scheming
acting as a playwright

I knew the song you were singing
before you even opened your mouth

a story of stars and alchemy and adventure

now I run towards thunderstorms
reinventing myself, being reborn
rejuvenating, renewing
mixing love and infusing
I've found the greatest clarity
after testing my vitality
and feel more alive than ever
when I know that every storm I can weather

Starlight Heart | Elise

I knew you long before I ever met you

Starlight Heart | Elise

in dreams tonight,
even if my mind has forgotten
my heart remembers

my lips are thirsty for the taste of you again

cathedral songs
the glass is singing
when the sunlight shines through
ring the bells
sound the bugle
a notion come true
in the towers in your heart
this time I'll place my faith in myself

Starlight Heart | Elise

why would I not carry
the art of my soul
on my skin always

Starlight Heart | Elise

bonfire heart,
igniting sparks
in the shadows
you are always bright
never fear the gallows
you are friends with the night

Starlight Heart | Elise

I walk these empty halls
with candle lights on the walls
broken hearts and worn out souls
I was there when the stories were told

everything fell away and I was left alone
in the dark, a single candle to hold
and that fire was my purpose
the one thing embedded into my soul
hold on to the light inside
sow the seed
do the deed
on midnight's horses we'll ride

a realisation sank into my bones that night
as I sat in the castle inn, listen to my soul
the words that had been buried underneath
suddenly were made of golden thread
and I couldn't pretend they weren't there
so say goodbye to the girl you once were
for tonight we drink to transformation

in a single moment
you can draw from all
you have ever known
information is surging
through pathways
in your brain
like electricity
in a circuit board
connect your thoughts
switch on your mind

Starlight Heart | Elise

I am a story in a castle
mighty walls unwavering
built with stones and dreams
and wild autumn things
clouds carry messages
over the hill
and late-night spectres
roam the villages
do I want a fairytale
the ones I was told
before sleep at night
or do I want a story

dragonfly in amber
voices in stone
what do you remember
soul and bone

at dusk we walked to the ruins of a castle
how strong we are to rebuild ourselves
and still be standing
if we wait long enough
the spirits will come out to play
great halls with fires and ghost stories
surround us in these hollow halls

Starlight Heart | Elise

if the stars in my heart sing for something
then by all means possible
I must learn the
lyrics to the song,
and play the melody of the music
until I become a composer myself

like the seasons of the world
maybe a part of you had to die
to be transformed and for
something new to bloom

•

Starlight Heart | Elise

will the stars give me wisdom
or will the sound of my own heart
tell me what I need to know

can I share with you the words in my heart?

butterfly with wings of ivory
forged in starlight fire
midnight blue
wings dripping in the universe
you sound like success

if you could bottle up the mindset of success
it would be valued at priceless

deal the cards for me card dealer of the carnival
with skulls tattooed on your knuckles
and ruby amulets dangling from your neck
tattered and burnt ebony black suit
and a top hat tilted to cover your face
smell of smoke and deeds done in darkness
but here I sit, as the clock tick's half past 1
in the inn along the road of no return
asking to play one more time

Starlight Heart | Elise

black wolf, fur as dark as night
haunt my dreams,
strength dripping from your back
still those soft celestial eyes
pierce into my soul
I don't know why,
but I trust you
or perhaps I do know why
you're a manifestation in my mind
and I'm trusting myself again

empyrean goddess in the sky
elysian dust
clouds of blue portals and other realms
detonate and encapsulate your spirit

Starlight Heart | Elise

now I carry my own tank of oxygen
life force
a chamber I keep in my pocket
charged full of starlight
for the darkest of nights

Starlight Heart | Elise

I came across a hut
in the jungle of my mind
violet smoke was billowing
out the chimney
and the door was locked
night-time crickets
sang a song of remembering
and inside were all the fables
and sagas of my youth

it became her ritual
to get tattooed on her a symbol
a word of ancient meaning to herself
to signify the pain she'd been through
that she had survived and that
she belonged intensely to herself
before anyone else

Starlight Heart | Elise

they listened to the words
and as they watched
the arches of her mouth
the lines of her lips
it was not air parting
from her lungs
but stardust

Starlight Heart | Elise

she was every bit a masterpiece of
original value
as she stood there against
the backdrop of the night sky
I didn't know where the
stars began, and she ended

•

the struggles don't get easier
you just learn to paint
armour on your skin

the deepest wound you gave me
a wound in my mind and heart
every time I think of a memory
it feels like the poison from the blade
is sinking deeper into my organs
there is no antidote
the only way to survive now
is to become stronger than the poison
an elixir unto myself

she is so in tune with the music of the world
I'm sure the universe wired her mind differently

as we lay next to each other
body to body
the cosmical dust that shone
through your veins
matched with the dust in mine
like a painting that was
lit with a lightning bolt

a union of souls under the summer sky

she poured the universe in a cup
and drank deep of the mysteries
that toiled in her mind night after night
most of all the mystery of her heart

Starlight Heart | Elise

if I were born by the blue flames in the sky
fire fox flickers in the torches in my eyes
what if I planted the dream in me from the start
and I gave myself a starlight heart

escape from the ordinary
it's not for me
I'm built from a different story

Starlight Heart | Elise

lightning fox, you run into the forest
tail dragging magic dust for me to follow
did you get the note from my mind
never look back at what's behind

midnight fire fox
hum me a tune
music of the stars
shines in your eyes
guardian of the forest
watcher in the woods
you've mapped the world
and know your way on the ground
but your home is the sky
and you play in constellations

writers dance with a distinct flame

Starlight Heart | Elise

the stories that start
in the stardust in my bones
more than a feeling
I've ever felt before
strange kind of magic
when imagination
feels like truth

and at last the words,
the rhyme, the story
burst out of my soul
like a firework of sounds
oil paintings in the sky
electric lights
neon signs

orchestra of lost souls
who can't sleep at night
because of dreams so big
your tummy turns
with anticipation
the next level
drummers drumming
a different tune
through the universe

telling stories
this is my domain

midnight train to
imagination's rule
divination in creation
beautiful

it's your choice
desire the electricity
that runs through your heart
be the defibrillator
apply your electric current
and change your course
with new life
and a new you
or die this way

my heart had weathered the storms
for so long and finally the sunlight
electrically charged my heart
and I felt new and alive again

Starlight Heart | Elise

stood atop the cathedral ruins
fairies in the breeze past my gaze
long blonde hair joins with
the winds of transformation
and you can smell the electricity in the air
as it tinges your skin
you can almost touch it
change is upon her like a ship wreck
rising from the bottom of the ocean
and she's taken back the helm

rebuild, everything is singing,
re-adjust your antenna to
pick up the signal of life
you want to dance with

Starlight Heart | Elise

no thank you to a normal life
I want to find out how much
I can ignite the sparks in my heart
and how ferocious they burn
and then I want to dance with them
into the witching hour
race with the stars
and greet the sunrise

the road is wide open now

Starlight Heart | Elise

I went to the oak tree to talk
I can't lie to him, to nature
because it's like lying to myself

keep the home fires burning darling

out in nature's monastery
I can think with clarity

Starlight Heart | Elise

closes her eyes
and goes into the universe
inside her mind

do you understand what I mean
when I say I have to do this or I'll die
my soul will die, my spirit will die
while my body still walks this world
a shell to my true potential
what life is that? No life of mine

emerge from the storm alone
and in the depths of your soul
you'll smile because you
know how strong you are

momentous dreams
a plan of action
starlight streams
build momentum
constant traction

Starlight Heart | Elise

let me soak in all the sweat of the universe
in pursuing my goal
let me get covered in the sparkles of lightning
that burst from my veins
when I'm getting closer and closer
and I know it
let me be drenched in the feeling
of pure trust in myself because I have not
let myself down
and the substance of my heart is visible
on my skin
a painting that symbolises the feeling of my heart

Starlight Heart | Elise

two goldfish in the deep blue sky
with glitter on their scales
swimming in a sea of
translucent stars

Starlight Heart | Elise

I'll drown before I learn
to breathe underwater
I'll fall before I learn
to fly
in failure I'll learn
and then I'll win

brew in a cauldron a mixture
of everything you are and
desire to become
it tastes of nectar's sweets
it sounds of winter's song
it smells of warm embers
it looks like the magic that runs
through your veins
and feels like the beginning of everything

Starlight Heart | Elise

I'll never be afraid of the story
I've got Viking blood in me

sail my ship into the unknown
and treacherous waters of my mind
in the sea voyages of life
one thing is certain
you won't come back the same

flowers falling
from the sky
set it on fire
and watch
the flames devour
what you once knew
and rebuild a kingdom
of vines and evergreens
plant the seeds
and watch the
blossom bloom

Starlight Heart | Elise

water fountains of stars
pouring from my heart
bleeding for the
memory of you
but no matter how much
I cover the thought
of you in stardust,
it won't disguise
the song of yours
that has left behind
something in my heart,
your music
and the sound of your soul
are all I have left of you

it hurts like a thousand cuts over my heart
it hurts like my soul has been torn into
it hurts like breath can't fill my lungs
there's some sort of release in the pain
because my head is saying
from here it can only get better

running, running miles through forests until my lungs
are burning and each breath is tough to breathe
because then in the pain there's another feeling
that tomorrow I'll be stronger than today

Starlight Heart | Elise

I'm one of those
who enjoy the pain of getting a tattoo
the pain of permanent change
a heart changes and your body listens
blood must be spilt, one way or another

could it be true
that two minds
share a heart
a soul that flows
fluidly between
two people

she picks ideas out of the air
like she can see the golden
air waves pulsating around her
and she chooses the idea
like a light bulb
like choosing which sweets to eat
to get a sugar rush in her mind
and from the light of an idea, get high

heal the hurt in your heart
nothing else can save you
but the voice inside your head

the seeds you sow in your soul
you will reap in your body

a garden of flowers grows in her heart

Starlight Heart | Elise

boom boom, boom bloom
a flower exploding from deep buried roots
on and on she grows her tower
a flower that blooms with the stars
a flower that glows like starlight
mysterious forbidden things
trying to solve the mysteries
when she forgot the mystery of her heart
conquer yourself first inscribed in her mind
we all have our demons and dragons
our darkest night of the soul
but we will all still bloom

she had a glimpse of something about her
as she walked by
she had something like sunlight
shimmering on her arm
bright colours of gold and blue
in the shape of a fox
peering beneath the surface

Starlight Heart | Elise

what if our souls
showed their truest
counterparts on our skin
what pictures would yours be?
hers, the girl with the stars
in her veins
her soul would be
a midnight fox

she's in a consistent mind of blooming

Starlight Heart | Elise

the words ripped me to my core
the pain deeper than ever before
what a night for it of all nights
when mighty eagles are taking flight
I suppose I should celebrate this rite of passage
still, under the stars I will flourish and blossom
moments when I truly become a woman

whether by stars or by night
the stories she has inside her
will tumble onto paper
and breathe starlight

when does fear turn into courage darling
when we jump into the flames no matter
the outcome
because there's the indomitable spirit inside
that will never be broken by the outside

maybe a lot of wisdom has already been said
by the greats, by the philosophers in stone
by the innovators and inventors
by the discoverers of hidden things
maybe they learnt from life and became wise
but wisdom can be said in another way
a way that resonates with your soul
a way that sings with you

I need wide open spaces
hilltop of ruins
scatter the ashes of my former life
into the wind
mourn the girl I was with you
now step into the woman I have become

bruised heart
you will hum
for the battles won
and carry wisdom
from the loss
victories are only sweet
because you know
the sour taste of failure

we've become warriors
we've become giants unto ourselves
and now we salute the electric pulse
that keeps our hearts beating
because we know it is ours

creating art from transforming energy
that can never be destroyed
so we transfer the energy of a thought in our mind
we draw it onto paper
we make it real with material things
how magical
to be an artist of transforming energy into
what you have imagined it could be

and I held on because I'd never felt this before
and I wanted to see how far it would go
and who I would be when we're finished
setting fire to each other's souls
and you set a fire in me when I was embers and ash
and I hoped we would never stop setting fires

there's a science and an art
to learning how to listen
to the things that
sing to your soul
and then running
with them

creation darling,
you smell of it

a tantalising performer on your stage tonight
you play the part you've been given well
a stellar actor by all means
I dare say you've learnt a trick or two
the next level you decide your character
and you'll mesmerise with your ethereal tones
on and on, you'll advance, a game well played
clap for yourself and take a bow

a wielder of wild imagination
a magician of sorts
or is that just what we call it
when a person knows
how to control the
energy in their mind

artistic freedom
explorations of a
cosmic mind

Starlight Heart | Elise

sing sweet soul
ready, ready, go

imprint and kiss
I was born for this

Starlight Heart | Elise

how did you make your soul?
bathed in sunlight
dripped in starlight
lit in flames
and painted with flowers

Starlight Heart | Elise

your heart is like mine
it skips a beat
when the stars come out

with her mind
she could
create melodies
maybe she wasn't
as much a myth
as we'd been
lead to believe
now I see her in flesh
I can touch her
and feel the electricity
that lives beneath her skin

you can get into someone's mind
more easily than you can get into their body

a soul remembers

a sight of two birds playing at sunset
could help heal a heart and a mind
surround yourself with beauty
and you will radiate warmth

the ones who pursue their goals
against all the hardships
who never lose sight of their dreams
and always live by their own heart
are the ones who get to taste
the sweetest nectar life has to offer

go on girl,
ignore the naysayers, the doubters
they are the ones who are left with
the sad realisation that they
didn't reach their potential
choose a side
lose or win

the fire alarm
went off every night
a call to arms
the smoke
from the flames
in my heart
got into the system
like ghosts in the
machine

Starlight Heart | Elise

cathedral of dreams
master of the orchestra in my heart
we were the lovers and I am the star

I'm in love with lyrics I haven't written yet

a melody written in the stars in my heart

when she hears the words in her mind
she hears them as songs and music
and each word she sings
and the symphony bursts
like explosions of light
illuminating frequencies along
pathways like never before

jump on the carousal of broken dreams
ride the horses to the streams
drink from your own water, it's not poison
let yourself bloom brighter than the night
dreams are only magic if you make them real

because it's not in some ancient book
where you'll find the truth about your soul
it's in pushing yourself to become
who you want to be
watering and feeding the spark in your heart
until it blooms into a wildfire
that can never be stopped
books are treasures
but life is a necessity

Starlight Heart | Elise

like a bomb that doesn't kill you
but makes you stronger
she couldn't be who she was any longer
she grows like a flower from the destruction
implementing herself, resurrection
now instead of boom, boom
she shines like boom bloom

Starlight Heart | Elise

I needed to get away
I went to stay in a shepherd's hut
to write some poems
and commune with the universe
away from the noise
out in nature
so I can hear my own voice sing to me

can you play with all the sounds of your heart
can you draw with all the colours of your soul

I thought I heard your voice on the wind

the electrifying art in her soul

Starlight Heart | Elise

she breaks into cathedrals at night
to sit and think and breathe
restless minds
rhythm and time
arranging elements by design
purposeful artwork by candlelight
what once was dark has become bright

be true to who you are
live in your song
you are your star
iridescent and strong

Starlight Heart | Elise

new cities bloom
spray painting
purple eyes on walls
eyes of night and stars
breathe life into the new
breathe life into your new self

ghost stories whisper to me in the cathedral walls
the revenant plays the organs quietly
melodies, he puts his story in the melodies

come on storyteller, tell us a story

Starlight Heart | Elise

I had no choice
it was come back home to myself and thrive
or wallow in misery and die
and I had not survived for this long to snuff out my own light

Starlight Heart | Elise

playing my own rendition
a new and brighter composition
of the music I can hear inside my mind
beautiful tapestry, so divine
light the way
your song has something to say

maybe I said love
was the best feeling
because I didn't know
what it felt like
to burn with the
true flames of authenticity

Starlight Heart | Elise

there's no need
to fear your dreams
when you sleep
if you know yourself
and the person you have become

as I read the words
written in her book
I kiss the pages and
hug the paper
I've never read anything
that quite sounds as
similar tune to my own
I have never met her
in real life but
I am sure we are
cut from the same cloth
because she seems to
write the poems I write too

renewal darling, you're vibrant with it

Starlight Heart | Elise

under the electric sky
we made love
as sparks fly
and it was the first time
I'd ever felt that alive
in someone else's arms
kiss your smile and charm
energy ever flowing together and apart
oh my love, what a connection of hearts

Starlight Heart | Elise

I want you,
but I want myself more
I need all of me
to become who I want to be

paint on her hands from drawing her picture
she was so much writing and art
that when she cried, her tears were not made of water
but of ink and paint

she'd rebuilt her bones with stories
her skin with illustrations and
the blood that flowed within
is ink and paint

what if the forbidden fruit is thinking your own thoughts and having the courage to follow through on them

she danced with darkness and flames in her eyes
and became the night she calls home

that unexplainable soul feeling
that keeps you awake at night

I realised I had to sing my song for myself first
before I could ever sing it to anyone else

Starlight Heart | Elise

that one song that plays on the radio
your song, that you play for you
at that exact moment driving along
the road in the mountains
is all the magic you need
from the universe that you're going
in the right direction

there's something in the air tonight
the jukebox is playing on repeat
spirits in the electricals
energy in the machine
neon signs flickering on the streets
what a time to be alive

my soul was starving for something elusive
and all those late-night songs, music was my soul food
and that summer I felt in my soul, more than I'd ever felt before

Starlight Heart | Elise

a story in a song
pick yourself up
and play on

swimming in the waters of the stars
diving into the dreams of all the stories
that feel like home

your song will live forever
you've put a piece of your soul in it

only you can sing your song darling

no longer the pretty girl
or the witty girl
but the woman
who never let the
fire in her go out

Starlight Heart | Elise

I can't explain it with words
but I'll play you a song
and you'll know

Starlight Heart | Elise

make love to me
like you've
known me forever
and kiss me like it's
the last time

the words came out in a melody
electrified in the air around me

Starlight Heart | Elise

I wanted you to know
I heard the song play
the very first time
I felt your heart
and have been listening to it
ever since

your voice could be as smooth as silk
but is your heart beating beautifully
for the words to carry meaning

singing words
and setting souls on fire

there is nothing more breathtaking
than the sound of someone's heart
when they're singing the song that
belongs to them

your soul plays the sweetest music for you
tune in

Starlight Heart | Elise

a poem in your smile
a song in your soul
a story in your heart
stars in your eyes

riding a musical wave

Starlight Heart | Elise

her soul is a fox
painted with stars
dancing in lightning
and singing poetry

Starlight Heart | Elise

watering the seeds in my garden with
starlight and heart music

be like the ever flowing
water of the stars
and know yourself
and all the light and dark
you are

harmonious symphony
a dance of the stars inside you
a journey for imaginative stoics

a mind like yours
is your most beautiful weapon
to becoming
your fullest potential

a woman of undeniable intellect
she took it upon herself to
shape her reality to what she wanted
and listened to her own mind

Starlight Heart | Elise

she listened to the
beat of her heart
and felt courage
she looked inside
and saw starlight

Elise x

Printed in Great Britain
by Amazon